W9-AWK-868

SHAUN

EXTREME SPORTS STARS

WHITE

BY MATT SCHEFF

SportsZone

An Imprint of Abdo Publishing
www.abdopublishing.com

www.abdopublishing.com

Published by Abdo Publishing, a division of ABDO, PO Box 398166,
Minneapolis, Minnesota 55439. Copyright © 2015 by Abdo
Consulting Group, Inc. International copyrights reserved in
all countries. No part of this book may be reproduced in
any form without written permission from the publisher.
SportsZone™ is a trademark and logo of Abdo Publishing.

Printed in the United States of America,
North Mankato, Minnesota
032014
092014

THIS BOOK CONTAINS
RECYCLED MATERIALS

Cover Photos: Michael Kappeler/picture-alliance/
dpa/AP Images (left); Sergei Grits/AP Images (right)
Interior Photos: Andrew Milligan/Press Association
via AP Images, 1, 26, 26-27; The Canadian Press,
Darryl Dyck/AP Images, 4-5; Kyodo via AP Images,
6, 13; Gerry Broome/AP Images, 7, 30 (right);
Ervin Monn/Shutterstock Images, 8; NatalieJean/
Shutterstock Images, 9; Mike Groll/AP Images,
10-11; Haslam Photography/AP Images, 12;
Douglas C. Pizac/AP Images, 14-15; Chris Polk/
AP Images, 16; Jerome T. Nakagawa/AP Images,
17; Mark Duncan/AP Images, 18-19, 30 (left); Mark
J. Terrill/AP Images, 20-21; Sean Kilpatrick/AP
Images 22-23, 31; The Denver Post, RJ Sangosti/
AP Images, 24-25; Jae C. Hong/AP Images, 28-29

Editor: Chrös McDougall
Series Designer: Maggie Villaume

Library of Congress Control Number: 2014932913

Cataloging-in-Publication Data
Scheff, Matt.
 Shaun White / Matt Scheff.
   p. cm. -- (Extreme sports stars)
Includes index.
ISBN 978-1-62403-455-8
1. White, Shaun, 1986- --Juvenile literature. 2. Snowboarders--
United States--Biography--Juvenile literature. I. Title.
796.939092--dc23
[B]
                                        2014932913

CONTENTS

VICTORY LAP

Shaun White appeared at the top of the halfpipe. The crowd roared. The world's most famous snowboarder was about to begin his first run at the 2010 Olympic Winter Games in Vancouver, Canada.

Shaun landed trick after trick. He started with a backside air by sailing into the air and grabbing the backside of his board. He followed that with a series of amazing big-air spins and flips. He landed every one of them. The judges gave him a score of 46.8. The highest possible score in snowboard halfpipe is 50.

Shaun White flies through the air during the 2010 Olympic Winter Games.

A special camera shows Shaun's movements through the air at the 2010 Olympics.

FAST FACT

Shaun calls his Double McTwist 1260 "The Tomahawk."

scheduled to be the last one. But no one before him could match Shaun's score. He could have skipped his second run and still won the gold medal. But Shaun wanted to put on a show. So he did what snowboarders call a "victory lap."

The victory lap was nearly perfect. This time, Shaun finished with a brand new trick. He launched into the air for a Double McTwist 1260. He flipped twice and spun three and a half times before landing. The crowd went wild. His score of 48.4 was the highest in Olympic history.

Shaun celebrates after securing the gold medal at the 2010 Olympics.

Shaun Roger White was born September 3, 1986, in San Diego, California. Shaun was not a healthy baby. His heart had not developed quite right in the womb. Shaun had to have two heart surgeries while he was very young.

Shaun takes flight at a 2009 tournament.

Shaun gets big air during a 2010 competition in California.

FAST FACT

Shaun's heart condition is called Tetralogy of Fallot. It affects approximately 5 in 10,000 babies.

Sprint

Sprint

YAHOO!

BUD LIGHT

XBOX 360

VISA

VISA

Shaun's surgeries worked. Soon, he was a healthy, energetic boy. He loved to play with his older brother, Jesse. They surfed, skied, and practiced skateboarding tricks.

Shaun started to snowboard when he was around six years old. He learned by watching Jesse and his father. Soon, Shaun was tearing down the mountains on his own.

Shaun greets fans during the 2012 US Open Snowboarding Championships in Vermont.

Shaun entered and won his first snowboarding contest at age seven. He went on to dominate youth snowboarding divisions. His ability to get big air set him apart from all the other riders.

Snowboarding was expensive. And Shaun wasn't making any money in amateur events. So in 2000, at age 13, he decided to go pro.

Shaun receives his gold medal after winning a 2010 US Snowboarding Grand Prix event.

halfpipe at the 2010 Olympics.

FAST FACT

Shaun's nicknames include "Animal" and "The Flying Tomato."

vancouver 2010

SHAUN WHITE

Some people called Shaun "Future Boy." They thought he was the future of snowboarding. But Shaun's pro career started with a disappointment. Many thought he could win halfpipe gold at the 2002 Winter Olympics in Salt Lake City, Utah. But Shaun didn't even make the US team.

Shaun bounced back. In 2003, he became the youngest rider ever to win the US Open slopestyle competition. He also won two gold medals at the Winter X Games.

Shaun competes in a 2001 World Cup event in Park City, Utah.

FAST FACT

Forbes magazine said Shaun was tied for the highest-paid athlete at the 2010 Winter Olympics.

FAST FACT

The ESPN television network
awarded Shaun the ESPY Award for
Best Action Sports Athlete in 2003.

Shaun was also a talented skateboarder. So he went pro in skateboarding as well. He went on a tour with skateboarding legend Tony Hawk. He watched how Hawk and other pros skated.

Shaun proved he was ready at the 2003 X Games. He took sixth place in the skateboarding vert event. It was an amazing achievement. The other X Games competitors were full-time skateboarders.

Shaun poses as he walks the red carpet during the 2003 ESPY Awards.

Shaun suffered a knee injury in 2004. He missed most of the year. However, he did win the Winter X Games slopestyle title that year. And he was even stronger at the 2005 Winter X Games. He scored an amazing 93 out of 100 to win the slopestyle gold medal. It was his third gold medal in a row in the event.

Shaun went to Italy for the 2006 Winter Olympics. He won the snowboard halfpipe gold medal with a score of 46.8.

FAST FACT

Shaun has an endorsement deal with Burton Snowboards. Burton makes a line of snowboards and clothing with Shaun's name on them.

Shaun takes a run in the halfpipe at the 2006 Winter Olympics.

Shaun chats with late-night TV host Jay Leno after winning an Olympic gold medal in 2006.

MAKING HISTORY

Shaun was the most famous action sports star in the world. Huge crowds followed him to every event. He was on magazine covers. He even helped develop his own snowboarding video game, *Shaun White Snowboarding*. In 2007, Shaun made history. He won gold in the skateboard vert event at the summer X Games. That made him the first athlete to have won gold at both the winter and summer

Shaun rides in an early round at the 2010 Olympics.

FAST FACT

Shaun played the voice of Clueless Smurf in the 2013 film *The Smurfs 2*.

Shaun badly wanted to win another gold medal at the 2010 Winter Olympics. So he had his own private halfpipe built. There, he could practice without any of his competitors seeing his moves.

The practice paid off. Shaun was almost perfect at the Olympics. He easily won his second consecutive Olympic gold medal.

Shaun just kept winning on the snow and the pavement. In 2011, he won gold at both the X Games and the Winter X Games. In 2012, he became the first person ever to score a perfect 100 in the Winter X Games snowboard superpipe event. And he won the superpipe again in 2013. It was the sixth straight year he earned gold in the event.

Shaun jumps over a huge gap during a slopestyle practice at the 2011 X Games.

FAST FACT

Shaun didn't compete in any skateboarding events in 2013. He wanted to focus on preparing for the 2014 Winter Olympics.

Shaun had high hopes for the 2014 Winter Olympics. At age 27, he was the favorite to win a third gold in halfpipe. Shaun was also expected to battle for a medal in slopestyle. That event was new to the Olympics.

The Olympics in Sochi, Russia, did not go well, however. Shaun dropped out of the slopestyle event before it started. He said he wanted to avoid injuries and focus on halfpipe. No one had ever won three Olympic snowboarding gold medals. Shaun started out with a thrilling run in qualifying. But he struggled in the finals. He stumbled several times on his final run and finished fourth.

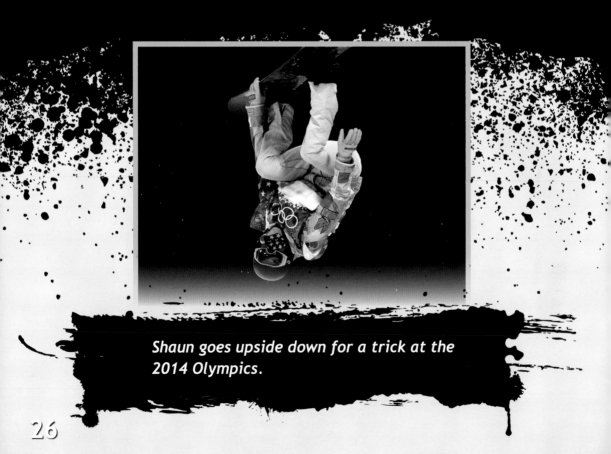

Shaun goes upside down for a trick at the 2014 Olympics.

A missed landing causes Shaun's snowboard to bend at the 2014 Olympics.

Shaun flies high above the halfpipe at the 2014 Olympics.

Shaun continues to amaze fans with his skill and his ability to push limits. His accomplishments in snowboarding and skateboarding make him unique. Few people have the ability to compete at the top of even one sport. Doing so in two different sports makes Shaun one of the greatest action sports stars of all time.

FAST FACT

Shaun is also a musician. He plays guitar in the rock band Bad Things.

TIMELINE

1986
Shaun is born on September 3 in San Diego, California.

1993
At age seven, Shaun enters and wins his first snowboarding contest.

2003
Shaun wins his first two Winter X Games gold medals.

2006
Shaun wins gold in the halfpipe competition in the Winter Olympics.

2007
Shaun becomes the first athlete to win gold in both the summer and Winter X Games.

2010
Shaun wins his second Olympic gold in the halfpipe.

2013
Shaun wins his sixth straight gold in the Winter X Games superpipe event.

2014
Shaun's quest for a third Olympic gold medal falls short when he finishes fourth in halfpipe.

GLOSSARY

amateur
A person who is not paid to compete in a sport.

endorsement
An agreement for a famous person to be paid to promote a company or product.

halfpipe
A type of ramp used in snowboarding and skateboarding, shaped like the letter U.

pro
Short for professional; a person who is paid to compete in a sport.

rider
Another word for someone who snowboards.

slopestyle
A snowboarding event in which riders complete tricks off jumps and rails on a terrain park.

superpipe
A type of snowboarding halfpipe that is wider than normal halfpipes, with high, vertical walls on both sides.

Tetralogy of Fallot
A condition in which the heart is formed abnormally, leading to a lack of oxygen in the blood.

vert
Short for vertical; in skateboarding, vert is a type of event held on a halfpipe with tall, vertical walls.

INDEX